VIRTUAL
REALITY

Other books by Bob Perelman

Braille
7 Works
a.k.a., parts 1 & 2
Primer
a.k.a.
To The Reader
The First World
Face Value
Captive Audience

VIRTUAL REALITY

BOB PERELMAN

ROOF BOOKS • NEW YORK

Design by Deborah Thomas.

ISBN: 0-937804-49-5
Library of Congress Catalog Card No. : 92-63354

Acknowledgements:
Versions of these poems have appeared in *Abacus, Aerial, The Archive Newsletter, Avec, The Best American Poetry, Epoch, Fuse, New American Writing, The Painted Bride Quarterly, Poetics Journal, Postmodern Culture, Shiny, Six, Sulfur, Temblor, Verse, The Wallace Stevens Newsletter,* and *Writing.* Thanks to all involved.

"Chronic Meanings" was written to and for Lee Hickman when I heard that he had AIDS. He published it in the last issue of his magazine, *Temblor.*

For Francie, Max, and Reuben

This book was made possible, in part, by grants from the New York State Council on the Arts, the National Endowment for the Arts and other generous donors.

Roof Books are published by
Segue Foundation
303 East 8th Street
New York, New York 10009

CONTENTS

VIRTUAL REALITY

It was past four when we
found our feet lifted above our

accelerators, only touching them at intervals.
Inside, our car radios were displaying

the body of our song, marked
with static from Pacific storms. Outside

was the setting for the story
of our life: Route 80 near

Emeryville—fence, frontage road, bay, hills,
billboards changing every couple of months.

It was the present—there was
nothing to contradict this—but it

seemed stopped short, a careless afterthought,
with the background impossible to keep

in focus. We weren't pleased with
the choices, words or stations, and

our desire pouted in the corners
of our song, where it clung

self-consciously to the rhythm-fill or bass
or the scratch in the voice

as it pushed the big moments
of the lyrics over the hump.

We were stacked up and our
path was jammed negotiation for every

forward foot. Hope of automatic writing,
of turning the wheel freely in

a narrative of convincing possibility, was
only a byproduct of the fallen

leaves lifted in the ads and
drifting sideways in slow motion as

the BMW cornered away from us
at forty. We were recording everything,

but the unlabeled cassettes were spilling
over into the footage currently being

shot. This was making the archives
frankly random. A specific request might

yield a county fair displaying its
rows of pleasures: candy apples, Skee-Ball,

two-headed sheep, the Cave Woman. She
looked normal enough, standing in her

plexiglass cage as the MC spieled:
the startled expedition, capture, scientific analysis.

But suddenly she interrupted him, breaking
her chains, thumping the glass and

grunting, as a holograph of a
gorilla was projected more or less

over her. The MC turned his
mike up and shouted, "We can't

control her!" and the lights went
out, which apparently was the signal

for us to stumble out of
the tent, amused, every hour on

the hour, gypped certainly, but possibly
a bit nostalgic. We had already

fashioned nooses out of coded nursery
twine to help the newscasters with

their pronunciation, and whipped up stampedes
of ghost dancers from old westerns,

not that we could see them.
If we lived there, in separate

bodies, we'd have been home long
ago, watching the entertainment morsels strip

and hand over everything, and telling
the dog to sit and not

to beg. But the more commands
we gave our body the more

it gaped and clumped together, over-excited
and impossible to do anything with.

We turned to analysis, negotiation, persuasion,
cards on the table, confession, surrender.

But there was no refamiliarizing. Our
machines filled the freeway with names

and desires, hurling aggressively streamlined messages
toward a future that seemed restless,

barely interested. We could almost see
our hands seizing towers, chains, dealerships,

the structures that drew the maps,
but there was no time to

read them, only to react, as
the global information net had become

obsessed with our body's every move,
spasm, twitch, smashing at it with

videotaped sticks, validating it, urging instant
credit, free getaways, passionate replacement offers.

THE MARGINALIZATION OF POETRY

If poems are eternal occasions, then
the pre-eternal context for the following

was a panel on "The Marginalization
of Poetry" at the American Comp.

Lit. Conference in San Diego, on
February 8, 1991, at 2:30 P.M.:

———————————————

"The Marginalization of Poetry"—it almost
goes without saying. Jack Spicer wrote,

"No one listens to poetry," but
the question then becomes, who is

Jack Spicer? Poets for whom he
matters would know, and their poems

would be written in a world
in which that line was heard,

though they'd scarcely refer to it.
Quoting or imitating another poet's line

is not benign, though at times
the practice can look like flattery.

In the regions of academic discourse,
the patterns of production and circulation

are different. There, it—again—goes
without saying that words, names, terms

are repeatable: citation is the prime
index of power. Strikingly original language

is not the point; the degree
to which a phrase or sentence

fits into a multiplicity of contexts
determines how influential it will be.

"The Marginalization of Poetry": the words
themselves display the dominant *lingua franca*

of the academic disciplines and, conversely,
the abject object status of poetry:

it's hard to think of any
poem where the word "marginalization" occurs.

It is being used here, but
this may or may not be

a poem: the couplets of six
word lines don't establish an audible

rhythm; perhaps they aren't, to use
the Calvinist mercantile metaphor, "earning" their

right to exist in their present
form—is this a line break

or am I simply chopping up
ineradicable prose? But to defend this

(poem) from its own attack, I'll
say that both the flush left

and irregular right margins constantly loom
as significant events, often interrupting what

I thought I was about to
write and making me write something

else entirely. Even though I'm going
back and rewriting, the problem still

reappears every six words. So this,
and every poem, is a marginal

work in a quite literal sense.
Prose poems are another matter: but

since they identify themselves as poems
through style and publication context, they

become a marginal subset of poetry,
in other words, doubly marginal. Now

of course I'm slipping back into
the metaphorical sense of marginal which,

however, in an academic context is
the standard sense. The growing mass

of writing on "marginalization" is not
concerned with margins, left or right

—and certainly not with its own.
Yet doesn't the word "marginalization" assume

the existence of some master page
beyond whose justified (and hence invisible)

margins the panoplies of themes, authors,
movements, objects of study exist in

all their colorful, authentic, handlettered marginality?
This master page reflects the functioning

of the profession, where the units
of currency are variously denominated prose:

the paper, the article, the book.
All critical prose can be seen

as elongated, smooth-edged rectangles of writing,
the sequences of words chopped into

arbitrary lines by the typesetter (Ruth
in tears amid the alien corn),

and into pages by publishing processes.
This violent smoothness is the visible

sign of the writer's submission to
norms of technological reproduction. "Submission" is

not quite the right word, though:
the finesse of the printing indicates

that the author has shares in
the power of the technocratic grid;

just as the citations and footnotes
in articles and university press books

are emblems of professional inclusion. But
hasn't the picture become a bit

binary? Aren't there some distinctions to
be drawn? Do I really want

to invoke Lukacs's "antinomies of bourgeois
thought," where rather than a conceptually

pure science that purchases its purity
at the cost of an irrational

and hence foul subject matter we
have the analogous odd couple of

a centralized, professionalized, cross-referenced criticism studying
marginalized, inspired (i.e., amateur), singular poetries?

Do I really want to lump
The Closing of the American Mind,

Walter Jackson Bate's biography of Keats,
and *Anti-Oedipus* together and oppose them

to any poem which happens to
be written in lines? Doesn't this

essentialize poetry in a big way?
Certainly some poetry is thoroughly opposed

to prose and does depend on
the precise way it's scored onto

the page: beyond their eccentric margins,
both Olson's *Maximus Poems* and Pound's

Cantos tend, as they progress, toward
the pictoral and gestural: in Pound

the Chinese ideograms, musical scores, hieroglyphs,
heart, diamond, club, and spade emblems,

little drawings of the moon and
of the winnowing tray of fate;

or those pages late in *Maximus*
where the orientation of the lines

spirals more than 360 degrees—one
spiralling page is reproduced in holograph.

These sections are immune to standardizing
media: to quote them you need

a photocopier not a word processor.
In a similar vein, the work

of some contemporary writers associated more
or less closely with the language

movement avoids standardized typographical grids and
is as self-specific as possible: Robert

Grenier's *Sentences*, a box of 500
poems printed on 5 by 8

notecards, or his recent work in
holograph, often scrawled; the variable leading

and irregular margins of Larry Eigner's
poems; Susan Howe's writing which uses

the page like a canvas—from
these one could extrapolate a poetry

where publication would be a demonstration
of private singularity approximating a neo-Platonic

vanishing point, anticipated by Klebnikov's handcolored,
single-copy books produced in the twenties.

Such an extrapolation would be inaccurate
as regards the writers I've mentioned,

and certainly creates a distorted picture
of the language movement, some of

whose members write very much for
a if not the public. But

still there's another grain of false
truth to my Manichean model of

a prosy command-center of criticism and
unique bivouacs on the poetic margins

so I'll keep this binary in
focus for another spate of couplets.

Parallel to such self-defined poetry, there's
been a tendency in some criticism

to valorize if not fetishize the
unrepeatable writing processes of the masters

—Gabler's *Ulysses* where the drama of
Joyce's writing mind becomes the shrine

of a critical edition; the facsimile
of Pound's editing-creation of what became

Eliot's *Waste Land*; the packets into
which Dickinson sewed her poems, where

the sequences possibly embody a higher
order; the notebooks in which Stein

and Toklas conversed in pencil: these
can make works like "Lifting Belly"

seem like an interchange between bodily
writers or writerly bodies in bed.

The feeling that three's a crowd
there is called up and canceled

by the print's intimacy and tact.
In all these cases, the unfathomable

particularity of the author's mind, body,
and writing situation is the object

of the reading. But it's time
to question or dissolve this binary.

What about a work like *Glas*?
—hardly a dully smooth critical monolith.

Doesn't it use the avant-garde (ancient
poetic adjective!) device of collage more

extensively than most poems? Is it
really all that different from, say,

the *Cantos*? (Yes. The *Cantos*'s growing
incoherence reflects Pound's free-fall writing situation;

Derrida's institutional address is central. Unlike
Pound's, Derrida's cut threads always reappear

farther along.) Nevertheless *Glas* easily outstrips
most contemporary poems in such "marginal"

qualities as undecidability and indecipherability—not
to mention the 4 to 10

margins per page. Compared to it,
these poems look like samplers upon

which are stitched the hoariest platitudes.
Not to wax polemical: there've been

plenty of attacks on the voice
poem, the experience poem, the numerous

mostly free verse descendants of Wordsworth's
spots of time: first person meditations

where the meaning of life becomes
visible after 30 lines. In its

own world, this poetry is far
from marginal: widely published and taught,

it has established substantial means of
reproducing itself. But with its distrust

of intellectuality (apparently synonymous with overintellectuality)
and its reliance on authenticity as

its basic category of judgment (and
the poems exist primarily to be

judged), it has become marginal with
respect to the more theory-oriented sectors

of the university, the sectors which
have produced such concepts as "marginalization."

As a antidote, let me quote
Glas: "One has to understand that

he is not *himself* before being
Medusa to himself. . . . To be oneself

is to-be-Medusa'd . . . . Dead sure of self. . . .
Self's dead sure biting (death)." Whatever

this might mean, and it's possibly
aggrandizingly post-feminist, man swallowing woman, nevertheless

in its complication of identity it
seems a step toward a more

communal and critical reading and writing
and thus useful. The puns and

citations lubricating Derrida's path, making it
too slippery for all but experienced

cake walkers are not the point.
What I want to propose in

this anti-generic or over-genred writing is
the possibility, not of some pure

genreless, authorless writing, but instead, a
polygeneric writing where margins are not

metaphors, and where readers are not
simply there, waiting to be liberated.

For all its transgression of local
critical decorum, *Glas* is still, in

its treatment of the philosophical tradition,
decorous; it is *marginalia*, and the

master page of Hegel is still
Hegel, and Genet is Hegel too.

But a self-critical poetry, minus the
short-circuiting rhetoric of vatic privilege, might

dissolve the antinomies of marginality that
broke Jack Spicer into broken lines.

FROM THE FRONT

This picture can hardly be right:
a man with a hammer upraised

above a grain of sand resting
on a glass table. Then there's

another thing wrong: a scowling man
pushing a baby in a carriage

while across the street a woman
holding a child in one arm

tries the houses, asking for work
on a balmy late fall afternoon.

While I rush through the conventionally
dim 'hallways', 'doors', and of course

up the stern 'stairs' of dreams
searching for the history exam offstage,

the ironies of permanent childhood uncover
themselves and gesture, their magic markers

falling and streaking all economic surfaces.
The color combinations in the catalogs

wither kaleidoscopically as the market refuses
to open its arms, reveal its

motives, or die in peace. It's
1991—at least it was, once

upon a time—and communism is
dead, leaving capitalism, the word, the

movie, the whole ball of idiomatic
wax, with nowhere to go, nothing

to mean. The free world belongs
in a language museum now, along

with free love and free verse.
In mainstream editorial cartoons Arabs have

big noses and big barrels of
oil, with real and emotional starvation

figured as dunes in a desert
that can't help being so dry.

On the freeways, in malls, in
bed, in couplets, the subjects of

history study, cut class, or flunk,
but no one passes. The soft,

cliched underbelly of consumer desire comes
on screen: the untensed bodies of

money incarnate, generic curls making hay
while the sun shines, the excised

pasts and futures formed into remnant
he's or she's whose job is

to demonstrate the willing suspension of
economic autonomy. In life, the actors

may be murdered, dead of AIDS
or the recombined by-products of industry,

or have gone back to school,
but nevertheless are there on cassette,

alive and moving, rented and possessed
in the shower with vibrator and

camera eye applied to the place
in the market which stands for

a particularly crude but still undefinable
hope for utopia. No escape from

the implosions of sitting and looking,
or looking away. My little horse

must think it queer. He gives
his harness bells a shake—we

are living in a permanent Christmastime
economy after all; so even if

it hardly snows anymore there are
plenty of harness bells—and suggests,

in a horsey way, that poetry
had better focus on coherent, individualized

spots of time, with a concomitant
narrative frame of loss. A carrot,

in other words, and not theoretical
sticks crashing down on parallel jargon-universes,

with the poet wearing self-critical armor
impossible to visualize, let alone read,

inflicting transpersonal wounds on the microarmies
of intellectuals organized into professional phalanxes.

On the battlefield, discipline is ragged,
and the lines separating the divisions

waver like metaphors on a foggy
spring evening, paired bodies, adolescent, in

love, buoyed on seas of plenty,
articulated by time and energy to

paroxysms of generosity, towards themselves if
no one else. But this is

to lecture the open barn door
well after the flying saucer has

disappeared over the horizon, taking understated
control of the airwaves, leaving behind

the smell of hay, the musty
charm of provincial dress and dialect.

These are the stuff of many
a mini-series, nor do the imaginary

raw materials of this poem-like writing
come from a separate world. The

poet has no job; the only
jobs now involve tracking classes under

glass, the stories accumulating spectacles of
damage. To write the histories with

any accuracy is to write backwards,
true to the falsity of experience.

There are no longer any individuals
or individual poems, only a future

more shattery than ever but still
nearer to us than the present.

Saw chairs back into branches, or
words and actions to that effect.

NEONEW

1.

possessing
possessing that
possessing that whose
possessing that whose loss
possessing that whose loss will be avenged
possessing that whose loss will be avenged by an unbroken history
    stretching backwards

1.

backwards into the body
into the body of the poor
the body of the poor Tatars
body of the poor Tatars Roman
of the poor Tatars Roman history
the poor Tatars Roman history intercalated
poor Tatars Roman history intercalated an alphabetic letter
Tatars Roman history intercalated an alphabetic letter they continue
    Tartars
Roman history intercalated an alphabetic letter they continue Tartars
    of fell Tartarean nature to this day

1.

entering the veins the law entering the veins

CHAPTERS OF VERSE

1. There are no poets in the natural order of things.

2. A world in which there are no last names and no families.

3. Each generation comes into existence by its own efforts, not through the sexual activity of its ancestors.

4. The physical present, death, eternity, type.

5. The kineticism of childhood seeks its own salvation behind society's back, in public suffers shipwreck and kitsch.

6. We are the moonlit sea.

7. We beat with thundering hoofs the level limiting conditions of a broadly legible social rhetoric widening itself on all sides, which sees, or thinks it sees, the roof above instantly receding, substance and darkness making up a canopy of shapes and tendencies to shape that shift and vanish, and shortly work less and less, until without effort or motion, the scene lies in perfect view, lifeless as a written book.

8. The scene lies in perfect view.

9. It is only in its resurrection that meaning dies.

10. Subjective workers kiss, not as lawyers, doctors, coast guard cadets, astronomers, sex therapists, or psychic healers.

11. Political language will get nothing but a mixed reception.

12. We, the public, with our dearest domestic ties, adopting our unseen hands as a free ride.

13. Human happiness is an image of relations in blood, binding up the constitution with fashion, melding close impossibilities into a timeless whole.

14. I do not believe poetry and prose will continue seven years longer.

15. When we, the two hundred and fifty million personal poets of the United States of America, have children whom we scarcely know what to do with, we make poets of them.

16. Images in blood.

17. The fact that the poet characterizes poetry as a church leads in a straight line to the founding of a language that goes beyond revolution towards a career of revelation.

18. A glimpse of an apostate son of a Quaker going to sea at sixteen; but the events of his biography lead in a straight line to the resurrection of the activity of his ancestors.

19. Experience is an accumulation of something like capital; but it is always in formation and if it is spent, it leaves the wind and sleety rain, the single sheep, the single tree dead from the wind, the bleak music of the old stone wall, the mist advancing on the intersection of two roads.

20. Uncommon language, loose parasitic body by centralization, acquires a range of daily content and real legibility, not in Utopia, in fields under the earth, or as some secret liberty of bypassing the objective conditions blocking our path, not as textual change in the world. As usual, prostitution is sacred, and universal.

21. There is not enough money to buy all the small-press books. And while there are more than enough diamonds to be the best friends of the eligible singles in the new releases, there are not enough releases to justify the building of the buildings of a new society. Thus poetry and

music limp along like aged friends, against a backdrop of real estate, under a sky of pure speculation.

22. Co-consumers seem perfectly willing to order from a diversity of catalogs. Omni-sectarians of desire ride the continent in search of the appropriate accreditation. Creeds and schools in abeyance.

23. To export need is to speak like a native.

24. Except for single words, there are no objects standing between the poet and revolution, and not just of literature alone, but of society as well.

25. The poet's mind when writing poetry is a mass of social individuals all using words at different times.

26. Poetry begins, not between individuals within a community, but rather at the points where communities end, at their boundaries, at the points of contact between different communities.

STATE HEADS

We the people, I the person, alive and haunting the discontinuum of
    bodies

Poetry in our time speaks in cars and air conditioners too constant for
    broadcast thought to say more than I see

Let there be headlines and there has to be filler

The President's head, sticking out of the sea on page 2, an absent rolling
    expression on the face, signifying nothing save shutter speed

The sinning son of a sod buster gone and got elected as a concrete
    universal

The President is the current one, the President of electricity, the
    President of particulate emissions and diamond vision, grass and
    dust, a motion surrogate dividing the landscape

Underneath the paper split pebbles of commercial nonsense bake in
    the sun, deleted by a light blue pencil or a dark red pen

Normal usage is the art of channeling weapons so the majority of
    sentences willingly enforce the current meaning of money with a
    minimum of state body revealed in the headlines

No sonic boom, more a slow drought and dubbed thought printed
    tonight and not allowed to age until tomorrow

In public and in fractions, jouissance delivered to responsible
    indviduals

A god's resume recognized at a glance

Terrorist-consumers struggling to eliminate the single word of slave prose

The poetic reader withers away

Some personal viewpoint tucked well under the freeway overpass with a story to tell and no one but the police to tell it to

Poetry and advertising, boardroom and bedroom, converge in the Wild West of governmental privacy

Jets above financial canyons the real picture of fictive capital

Sense-seeking words rived by career reading

Chernobyl was the kind of joke that makes poetry serious

Go back to the dawn of time, pick up a club and plot revenge, or wake up and smell the freeway burning

MONEY

I am I because my little dog knows me
— Gertrude Stein

Wallace Stevens says Money is a kind of poetry. So I offer to trade him Tennessee, States, and Water Works for Boardwalk and Park Place and the four Railroads. He thinks he'll pass. Do it I say and I'll quote you. Do says he. Mesdames, one might believe that Shelley lies less in the stars than in their earthly wake, since the radiant disclosures that you make are of an eternal vista, manqué and gold and brown, an Italy of the mind, a place of fear before the disorder of the strange, a time in which the poet's politics will rule in a poet's world. Yet that will be a world impossible for poets, who complain and prophesy, in their complaints, and are never of the world in which they live. Yes he says, gorgeous, I'm throwing in Pacific, North Carolina, and Pennsylvania. Go on. I can't I say. But do he says. Fair use I say. But all use is fair to one such as I says he, *con-tin-u-e*. No I say, 11 lines, any more and I'll have to write to Vintage, which I really don't want to do. But that's nothing he says, 11 lines out of 187. He says I'll give you Marvin Gardens, Ventnor, Atlantic.

That was the present, the poetic present tense: a non-financial play space, overheard.

Money has tenses: it has absolute meaning in the present; no past; and its future meaning (interest rates) reflects the degree to which the future is expected to resemble the present.

Writing has tenses: the past tense makes the most money (novels, reporting); the future is for prophecy (crop forecasts, pennant predictions); the present continually has to borrow credit. I am I because I say so and my little audience knows me.

Wow, says Basket. Wow, wow, wow!

How much money does it cost to know that Basket was a series of dogs owned by Gertrude Stein? Nothing, now.

I give I will give Basket the following bone (all past tense):

There was once a man, a very poor poet, who used to write poems that no one read. One evening, after working all day on an especially poor poem, he fell asleep in despair at the sterility of his imagination and the bleakness of his chances of making it as a writer. He had just typed the lines,

The sky was mauve and as far away
as a ten dollar bill.

He awoke with a start. The dim light from a small full moon was shining down at a forty five degree angle on his hands and the typewriter keyboard. He had slept two or three hours. Instinctively he looked up to the page—it was his last piece of paper—but it was gone. The moon shone on the bare roller.

Then he saw the page beside the typewriter. He must have taken it out before he dozed off, he thought. When he picked it up to put it back in the typewriter he noticed a small slip of paper sliding off the top— money! He stood up and snapped on the light. A real ten dollar bill, green and crisp!

He felt elated. His first reader! A realist who nevertheless appreciated his metaphors or similes or whatever they were! Real money!

Still inspired, the next morning he bought *The Selected Poems of Emily Dickinson* and two pieces of paper. That evening he wrote a careful twenty line poem and went to sleep expectantly.

The next morning: nothing.

He put his last piece of paper in the machine and began a poem.

The girl took twenty dollars from her mother's purse

was followed by forty nine more lines describing an approach to sex and the experience of alienation. It ended,

Dew beaded the windshield.

Sure enough, the next morning, there was a twenty dollar bill on the page, and a checkmark next to the final line, which he took to mean "Good."

34

He went out and bought *Ulysses* and *The Words* and, confidently, a single piece of paper. One was all he would need.

Late in the afternoon, he popped open a Bud and began to type away cheerily. He waited till he was two thirds of the way to the bottom of the page before mentioning the sum of forty dollars, which of course he received the next morning, the two twenties placed neatly on top of the page lying beside the typewriter. There was no checkmark, but he didn't mind so much. He did have a slight headache, from the beer.

Needless to say, he made lots of money. The checkmarks were irregular, and in truth not all that plentiful—many of what he thought of as his best passages remained checkless, while some of the low water marks apparently went over well—but he was pretty stoic about it. He was always paid in cash, even when he mentioned sums in five figures.

One day, when his library was almost complete—he had bought *My Life* and *Vice* that afternoon—he felt a strange stirring in his stomach or teeth or forearms, he couldn't pin it down. He wanted to shop. He grabbed the sixteen hundred dollars from the night before, stuffed it in his billfold, and went out to find a grocery store and an electronics store: food and TV, why not? He was productive, well off, his work was read. Why not relax?

His first stop was The Good Guys. He had a long talk with the salesman about the makes. It boiled down to Mitsubishi vs. Sony. He was naive but the salesman was there to help. He decided on a Sony. He wasn't going to get remote control, but it was part of the package. How was he going to pay? Cash, he said. He worried that it would draw a funny look, but it didn't. He reached into his pocket, and to his horror the bills he saw in his billfold were Monopoly money, two orange five hundreds, four yellow hundreds, and four blue fifties. He looked at the salesman, whose hair, he noticed, was exceptionally neat.

The poor poet thought of the sheet of white paper waiting for him in the roller. He had been thinking of getting a computer sometime soon but now he just wanted to get out of the store and relate to the somber physicality of the typewriter.

He had already waited a couple of seconds too long to pay. He gave the salesman an orange five hundred. "Where are you parked?" the

35

salesman asked, as he handed the sales slip and the bill to a woman at one of the cash registers. "Oh," said the poet, truly at a loss. "I didn't bring a car." "You can pick it up tomorrow," said the salesman, "just bring your sales slip."

Wow, says Basket, but only one wow.

I ask him about Gertrude. He says she wrote for money, too. Every word.

THE NET

some sort of   SOME SORT OF
separating process sexual   SEPARATING PROCESS IT'S
bulge bridge badge   SEXUAL AFTER THE
ways to win   FACT I KNOW I'M
eyes to the front   SECOND BUT I WANT
of the lit net   TO SAY WHAT YOU
material bodies   HEAR MOVE MY BODY
show through   ALONG YOURS AT ONCE
both so bad   HOPE DRIVES
they cut   ME TOWARDS
the net   YOU ALWAYS
when no one   HOPING TO GET
is watching   CLOSER ALWAYS
letting go   THINKING THE
not even herLONGER THE
say it with soundMORE
insiMOTIONLESS I
hear STAY HERE
in si WHERE I
NOW AM THOROUGHLY
ENTRENCHED bed
NEXT TOising those willful
YOU NEAR AT A children using
PARTICULAR DISTANCE those meaningful
FROM YOU   words to
TO STAY   stay in
IN TIME   touch sex
SEX THE   the fulltime
FULLTIME JOB   job these
THESE DAYS   days

CRITICAL PARTS

Subject: OBJECTIVE:

Jocasta—what made you

                                 WE SEE THE TRUNKS OF AN

say Jocasta?—makeup ten

                                 EMPTY FOREST HEAR A FLUTE

thousand years thick on her

                                 PLAYING MACDOWELL THEN

sixteen year old face no way

                                 A RIFLE EXTENDS WARILY

not to exaggerate there seem to

                                 INTO THE FRAME FOLLOWED BY

be no factual features beneath that

                                 ONE YELLOW BOOT TWO YELLOW

artifice an army of private investigators

                                 BOOTS RED PANTS TAN JACKET

combs the city, vengeance gives male birth to

                                 PLAID RED CAP COMPLETING

a nation with a body more real than any other and

                                 THE ENSEMBLE OF THE BULBOUS

why now this need to devour the landscape empty as a

                                 HUNTER WHO ARRIVES AND

broken bowl, glove on gearshift, punishing the motoroil

                                 IS ELMER FUDD HUSHING

thoroughly I push my body through the moving picture, to not

                                 THE VIEWERS LISPING HUSKILY

always have to worship at that altar that said No so long ago

                                 THAT HE'S HUNTING WABBIT

in the present I have to stretch hard to reach there's always the
                    ROADRUNNER IS ZOOMING ACROSS
future how can we tell the dancers from the ad in theory it's easy
                    TO THE LEFT. FROM ABOVE COYOTE
the cuts destroy the sentences this isn't school the effervescence
                    SLAMS A WASHTUB DOWN OVER
of the camera angles hits the bodies fast as interest rates change
                    RR'S TRAJECTORY AND JUMPS
their faces are recognizably different and the hair less so shot
                    ON TOP OF IT, LIGHTS
from all over dancing is a job their expressions are individually
                    A STICK OF DYNAMITE, LIFTS
identical being professional is a job what's nice is getting paid
                    THE TUB UP A CRACK, SHOVES
even for the outtakes we're seeing the real thing it's easy to tell
                    THE DYNAMITE IN, THEN WAITS
their bodies from the Pepsi they're selling in theory lighting more
                    SLUMPED OVER THE UPSIDE DOWN TUB
perfect than words record setting temperatures ice cold pleasure of
                    WITH HAPPY CLOSED EYES. RR
the right choice each picture pleasurably different effervescent Uh
                    ZOOMS UP FROM LEFT, STOPS
Huh Ray Charles is happy he gets the joke each time the same that's
                    AND STARES. C STARES BACK, ANTICIPATING
quality we see him wearing a big grin You Got the Right One up top
                    ROADRUNNER DONE TO A TURN
buy shares pleasure ice Ray Charles gets the joke it makes him like
                    BY THE CULINARY DYNAMITE. RR
to laugh out loud throwing his head back behind the pulsing Uh Huh
                    STICKS HIS TONGUE OUT, ZOOMS OFF
the letters in theory totally filling the screen a second the joke
                    LEFT. C DOUBLETAKES, JUMPS

I can see Uh Huh agrees with the white cold light brown a long joke
    OFF THE TUB, CROUCHES, PEERS
pleasure is not the word You Got the Uh Huh Right one hot syntax
    IN CRAWLS INSIDE TO SEE.
lights they're getting record setting theory filling the fact that
    HE STANDS UP WITH THE TUB ON
his song lasts two seconds is funny if told to the right person Ray
    HIS SHOULDERS, SHRUGS: NOTHING
Charles' signature sunglasses black tie optional this isn't school
    THERE BUT THE !LIT DYNAMITE! HE
light effervescent ice is a job for the right professional it's fun
    SQUASHES THE TUB OVER IT AS IT
the montage outflanks syntax 110% tasteful hair and nightclub decor
    EXPLODES, BLOWING HIM UP OUT OF
addressed to the eye that exists to read shares of theory fluently
    THE FRAME. WHEN HE COMES DOWN,
the price of filling time driving the bodies pleasure not the word
    THE TUB IS TIGHT AROUND HIS
to sell bodies letters throbbing forward almost filling the screen
    NECK, NOW 3/4 HIS HEIGHT.

Experience:

　　　　MEANING:

　　　　　　　　Theory:

the room echoes

　　　　THE TRICK CHAINED

　　　　　　　　a word for each meaning

in livid fealty

　　　　IN POSITION AESTHETICIZED

　　　　　　　　something big for

to instant registration

　　　　EXPERIENCE & POLITICIZED

　　　　　　　　mass

soaking up sense

　　　　SENSE THE WHITE DESIRE

　　　　　　　　simple perhaps sans serif

let me back up and tell of

　　　　TO HOSE THE STREETS

　　　　　　　　for autonomy

the time when I was

　　　　FURTHER WIDER THAN

　　　　　　　　a red word for

it was before

　　　　THESE VERBAL WORDS

　　　　　　　　red things and so on

damn I'm shouting at

　　　　HUMAN PERSONS

　　　　　　　　et cetera etc

the TV courtroom again

　　　　IN HISTORICAL DRAMAS

　　　　　　　　until justice reigns

is My Lai

　　　　THE FLESH I SELL MYSELF

　　　　　　　　in every sound

short for my life?

　　　　FOR A CONTROLLING INTEREST IN THE SIGN

.it is convenient. WHEN WE ARE IN PROSPERITY .that words exist. OH THE LITTLE THAT .therefore we speak. WE THINK OF .& mean them. SUCH DREADFUL SIGHTS .we will not give up. AND TO SEE .Star Wars till they, not to be. OUR DEAR FRIENDS & .confused with you, pry the cold. RELATIONS BLEEDING OUT THEIR .dead singularity from the vocabulary. HEARTS BLOOD .all missing parts. UPON THE GROUND .accounted for. THERE WAS .parsed. ONE WHO .allseeing. WAS CHOPPED .power rereads Emma in the Count's arms. IN THE HEAD .for the only time. WITH A HATCHET .the law illegal. STRIPPED NAKED .beneath my dress. AND YET WAS .rivers of white. CRAWLING UP AND DOWN .undermining the page. IT IS A SOLEMN .sad, oncological. SIGHT .but sexy at the right angle. TO SEE .poet sings reader hears. SO MANY CHRISTIANS .behind bars. LYING IN THEIR BLOOD .series of pleasures. SOME THERE .sold direct to the face. SOME HERE .for a plausible social life. LIKE .the stores. A COMPANY OF SHEEP TORN .classic, classy, chiselled, unchangeable. BY WOLVES .but quick to die. ALL OF THEM .with open arms & legs. STRIPPED .missing lives of 200,000 bodies. NAKED .diced to mulch. A COMPANY .the poetry around the white farmhouse. OF HELL-HOUNDS .that good night. ROARING .selling itself. SINGING, RANTING .to itself. AND INSULTING .frozen. AS IF .into identity frenzy. THEY .the most convulsively. WOULD HAVE .endless movie. TORN .aims its cuts. OUR VERY HEARTS .at the most. OUT YET .pointed. THE LORD BY HIS .customers. ALMIGHTY POWER .the dead man the controls. PRESERVED .locked. A NUMBER .brushed chrome &. OF US FROM .leather. DEATH .try to touch it. TWENTY-FOUR .more than synchronized with the fastest impression. OF US TAKEN .pessimism of the printed word. ALIVE .payable on demand. AND .the heavier the less deductible. CARRIED .optimism of the writing mind. CAPTIVE .bouncing off the bumperstickers.

PICTURE WRITING

Along the top of the canvas, these images in the shape of a rainbow:

Far left: blue sky bisected by Frank Sinatra's voice, a thick golden gouge repeated every thirty minutes until darkness falls. The irregular blue lozenges that remain are the stars. They twinkle.

Left: a man with a slight resemblance to George Bush sitting on a back porch mumbling some verses from St Augustine's *The Sun Is Gonna Shine In My Back Door Some Day*, his face orange under the flushes of wine and sunset.

Near left: a dark green lead soldier, wooden with excitement, feeling the sexuality of metaphor within himself for the first time, and shooting forward to meet his career goal, a human body with his name written all over it.

Center: a round meat patty, half cooked, sizzling on Freud's couch, the tiny bits of white gristle in the browning pink forming a pattern which turns out to be a ball of lead and a small child holding a flag being dropped simultaneously from the Leaning Tower of Pisa; on the flag is stitched a child's image of a sandcastle under construction; one hand rests on its side, while the other has just pushed its index finger through the wall, making a crude window; inside this window a bed can be made out dimly; two apparently naked figures with crowns on cannot be seen under the rich coverlet, half thrown off, billowing to the floor.

Near right: all that is solid melting into air, all that is gaseous condensing into grey fibrous solids and entering the liver of Jose Napoleon Duarte.

Right: twenty boys, ranging in age from six to ten, kneeling in a circle around a lifesize cutout poster of Orel B. Hersheiser IV. On the front of his uniform the words I LOVE and HE LOVES are inscribed in blue

43

across the chest, superimposed at right angles. The back of the poster is unprinted grey cardboard except for the words YOU LOVE also in blue where the uniform number would be.

Far right: the Washington Monument, emitting rhythmically from its tip a continuous ribbon of a film of the Meese Commission on Pornography in which ten men and two women are looking at video tapes and loops, and are thumbing through magazines. They occasionally talk to one another, while television cameras film them and reporters sit taking notes in the audience. The emitted ribbon of film swirls down around the Monument and beyond to wreathe the poem which is represented as written on an unrolled scroll of parchment in the center of the canvas below the images. Pink diapered Cupids slide down the slopes of film.

The title of the poem, "Pleasure," is painted in thick red letters, the body of the text in fine gold. There are some drips.

PLEASURE

                              Speaking
                          for the p
                    leasure of mov
                ing the pen from
              the top of an
            imaginary box s
          liding down and to
          the left leaving i
        n this case a blue
        trail from the poi
        nt at the base of
          the tube my finge
          rs grip still s
            liding the po
              int slight
                ly down
                    but now to
                        the right, havin
                          g bowed the left
                            -behind track out
                              then back to the l
                              eft and coming to a
                              stop at the bottom
                              of the imaginary b
                            ox now filled with
                            the capital S of
                        Speaking which
                    I'll write a
                last time for
          pleasure:
      Speaking

45

PRAISE & BLAME

I mean this says the written body a lame duck
a world without money still as a written line

I mean this says the written body a lame duck
market the results or at least publish them

a world without money still as a written line
distribution determines rank a literary word

without a past magazines printed at irregular
intervals don't remind me a constantly broken

market the results or at least publish them
distribution determines rank a literary word

intervals don't remind me a constantly broken
sequence of investments the imperfect tense I

was moving a chair hearing a clock tower ring
without a past magazines printed at irregular

I remember buying but not reading the Tibetan
Book of the Dead I've parted my hair the same

place since age ten the original word without
sequence of investments the imperfect tense I

was moving a chair hearing a clock tower ring
echo "younger than spring time" a sentimental

education is always one life too late so that
when the spectacle touches my body I'm slid

into the trench history's an umbrella made of
echo "younger than spring time" a sentimental

place since age ten the original word without
education is always one life too late so that

I remember buying but not reading the Tibetan
machines twenty clouds in the sky and all for

naught a problem the non-biodegradable future
will inherit with its characteristically bent

into the trench history's an umbrella made of
sense of purpose the date is grey in grey and

alive in a spread-sheet morguish way shows of
depth torching the human buildings twisted

place since age ten the original word without
depth torching the human buildings twisted

sequence of investments the imperfect tense I
dead satisfaction left never mind the feeling

intervals don't remind me a constantly broken
echo "younger than spring time" a sentimental

victory utter annihilation the body following
circular songs of praise and blame knit tight

depth torching the human buildings twisted
into the trench history's an umbrella made of

victory utter annihilation the body following
like a dog children wake in chapter eleven of

the Bhopal Trilogy men from Big Blue ride the
painted wooden helicopters above the hospital

crib no need to render details unto Caesar in
our lifetimes outtakes stand for authenticity

market the results or at least publish them
a world without money still as a written line

victory utter annihilation the body following
like a dog children wake in chapter eleven of

our lifetimes outtakes stand for authenticity
the Bhopal Trilogy men from Big Blue ride the

solemn confusion around the career trajectory
only authority can be present the audience is

free to attend as attendant nutshells dance a
solemn confusion around the career trajectory

shoehorning the credit-worthy fifteen million
into cars the face and the voice copyright in

solemn confusion around the career trajectory
machines twenty clouds in the sky and all for

dead satisfaction left never mind the feeling
painted wooden helicopters above the hospital

a world without money still as a written line
alive in a spread-sheet morguish way shows of

victory utter annihilation the body following
into cars the face and the voice copyright in

a world without money still as a written line
sense of purpose the date is grey in grey and

I mean this says the written body a lame duck
shoehorning the credit-worthy fifteen million

intervals don't remind me a constantly broken
Book of the Dead I've parted my hair the same

crib no need to render details unto Caesar in
circular songs of praise and blame knit tight

AUTOBIOGRAPHY BY APHORISM

The father was attempting to explain castration. "They say it's complete-
ly academic, but believe me, it's not. I'd like you to sit still for a second,
not squirm, not plug your ears, or make faces, or keep your face blank
either, and please just listen. Don't watch my mouth. This wasn't my
idea, either. Just assume a normal expression and maintain it out of cour-
tesy. History doesn't take place in your room, for you to lip synch. Mick
Jagger is a symbol of the death of aura. His sweaty face has the farce-fed
grandeur of all reruns of authenticity. Every sentence has a subject,
whether the sky's on fire, or the kettle is humming its little tune in time
to the daffodils. Do you want lift-off or just Brownian motion? One
comes after two. Rotate your utopia to line up with my body's time and
then we'll be able to skip the past tense in our family wagon—remorse
in every western—the problems the Smithsonian has with the color
adjustment of multiculturalism so close to the White House. Pick any
pebble. Better than Bartok, better than Proust? Remember how we
struck gold on the prairie but each grain was so heavy we couldn't even
lift our arms to turn off the radio to write America as one word? I gave
you your name, and your first word was the sound of a bullet ricochet-
ing. It was still hot at sunset and the air smelled almost like a kitchen.
There was a lake in the center of the distance, as concentrated a blue as I
ever hope to see. But it was like trying to settle in a giant's hoofprint. I
hope you're writing this down—multiculturalism is one word, Brownian
with a capital B. Are you even listening to me?"

>—*Extremely happy and extremely unhappy*
>*men are exactly alike.*

The one time I was in Paris I pawned my dictionary for a bronze model
guillotine. I only knew one person and my clothes were more uncon-
sciously provincial than I had ever been, which I had always been
proud of in a sneaky sort of way. Thought was total. I wrote sonnets:
my record was two minutes and forty-five seconds. They rhymed, too.

On commercial forays I employed staccato ellipses: des oeuf, pain. If I'd been a dog I probably would have looked for a lamppost. As it was I eked out my niche, and manicured its voids and insurgent symbols. It was the end of the beginning, the dumbshow of the gods, just for me, but since literature is signed by pragmatic rules, I quickly returned to America having written only ampersands for the reader to translate into a present tense.

> —The writer is the one
> who is always the author's favorite.

The milk bottle joke depends upon changed values given to "boy" and "mother." If time never stops, relative to the cultural capital spread across the desk in homely, personalized messes, then incomprehension becomes a kind familial response. Is it that you love your body, or do you just resent any question as to its being? The joke is the kind that brings in secondary characters, education and jobs, big wars which filter into the room and make the desk a place of high-powered consumption: caffeine, endless references. But it was an ill-starred attempt to escape mother, whose ghost brought the most inefficient gossip, every afternoon. He couldn't keep her out. The result was writer's block as we now say, a poor surface on which to scratch out the forms of his inmost desires, not to mention bringing them to careful fruition. Lifetimes later, a statue stands pointing out a grim city dawn, surrounded by detective slasher real estate prose whose solidified violence forms a track for the laughter that never comes. Morning pronouns comb through the crumbs, but it's too late. Breakfast is over.

> —There is a great difference
> between praise and blame.

If art is to remain heroic, and the nation a place that all young people willingly want to paint & breathe & compost in a serious way, then someone should write a screenplay where John Wayne, played by George Washington, meets W.E.B. Dubois, played by Spike Lee, crossing the Delaware, played by Molly Bloom or James Joyce. The question of who gets to discover what continent and where on each other they might find them would get the plot going and cuts, focus, gesture, and accent could take it from there. Underemployed autosexual ushers would hand the audience walkie-talkies to keep in touch, trade perceptions, and market impressions. Nature would issue its own banknotes. Black and white bodies on the melting icefloes beneath the ozone holes invisible behind the fog—if the theatrical climate could be kept cold enough, the old political narratives could be felt with the clarity of a test-pattern. There would be a heavy circle enclosing the public clash of vested, disembodied interests in the shape of an X or an I or an asterisk, providing a nexus of jobs and a circumference of emotive postures, and nothing else. The action would take place in the winter palaces of the audience's frozen breath.

> —*Most of the world's troubles come*
> *from making a mistake.*

The Titanic was a literary theme, Managua is not. Pinched nerves are geopolitical burdens. A man sees a name on a tag. So what's social life for if not changing channels? The movies have taught the viewing class to read a crocodile surging as a natural language. The hero is hardly eaten at all. You can leave the television on, do whatever you want. They can't see you.

> —*Terrorism is essentially the rage*
> *of literati at a banquet*

I used to harbor a conception of the self that derived from the day when I was two and looked up at the sky. It was full of clouds, a fleeting composition forming a euphemism for language. From that day (I have a postcard of my point of view framed by vines) I was free from all memorized vocabulary and the consequences of whatever apologies I might utter at school. A pleasure, transposing fate into style without having to worry about the failures in Genesis. A marxist tourguide of the Cataclysm showed me the wind, and where it integrates into factories and then into stinking creeks. Her analysis was sexual, and I thought it was right to read her thirst for community as inclusive.

—Nature never happens twice.

She reaches behind her neck to undo her pearls and habit, willing the moment to sleep. Obedience dreams of pressed precise glyphs, groupings, curves, wakeup calls under sunny trees, a plunge to obsession in the mire, classes where the units strip right down to the White House. But that is all hearsay. Meaning slips into something less natural.

—Nothing is more beautiful
  than being able to set a bad example.

A BODY

If a poem is a body
and desire is more than a

word, then I desire the body
of this poem, standing beyond these

words, naked, unwritten, teasing me by
addressing you, reader, judge and executioner

of my will, which I am
writing in public, counting to six

and watching lines pair, as I
want to experience this body of

writing word by word. If it
exhibits crime by writing learnedly ventilator,

it is to give you pleasure,
and an irrational return on your

reading investment, where eye- and back-
strain are real risks, not to

mention savage boredom at the evocation
of untoward echoes, a kitchen counter's

speckled formica unintentionally calling up flecks
of blood on prehistoric cave walls

or poorly washed floors in government
basements. A poem should offer steady

increases in meaning for the foreseeable
future; it could skyrocket like Impressionism

in the eighties. Poetry is a
pyramid scheme, an inverted one, whose

point flickers as I breathe, and
whose base is pinnacled, so to

speak, in the sky—technically, in
the intense inane: the concentrated vacuum

of linguistic openness. From that utopia,
along paths invisible to the present,

the roofless malls of a biomorphic
future earth will descend, offering test-sites

for syntax exhibitionists and narrative flashpoints
for weather fetishists—at least that's

what I was taught in school:
April is the cruelest month, breeding

lilacs out of the dead land,
mixing memory and desire. I remember

sitting in front of rectangular walls
and pages, occasionally identifying with the

revealed meanings but more often losing
myself in the distances. I learned

that there are two *l*'s in
cruellest, neither one the same; two

e's; an *r*, a *u*, an
s, a *c*; and a *t*:

some of the more evocative letters
in our arsenal of weaned sound,

endlessly murmuring their second generation truths.
The same lives and difference kills

and names it, that's how history
continues pronouncing this. The woman still

has a penis, but this penis
is no longer the same penis.

Something else has, so to speak,
been appointed its successor. The rise

of the intellectual fits in here,
but nobody can say exactly where

without the exactitude being guaranteed institutionally,
which then generates the problem of

an institution to report home to,
be in bed with, however chastely,

and to rise above in dreams.
In the focused but hypnotic specificity

of the self, the setting might
involve the dark tents of innumerable

students surrounding an illuminated opera house,
a nipple of light commanded by

the heights of the dream vantage.
Inside, the audience's employment is sacrificed

on performance night for the salvation
of the professionals. I celebrate myself,

and sing myself, and what I
assume you shall assume: a world,

whose collective eyes, tuned to mutually
provocative codes of pleasure, drop tears

as fast as the Arabian trees
their med'cinable gum. Set you down

this, and don't forget to specify
the funding lines to guarantee both

the kinks and the articulation of
the culture rubdowns that will, as

you say, somehow or other generate
those skyey malls I'm sure we're

all anxious to check out just
as soon as they're up and

running. But now, when we squint
upwards, bright bands of UV fall

from the air, irradiating the spectrum
and making national colors glow fiercely.

Not like the old days when
Kuwait or Chile or Guatemala would

play strip-poker in the Smiths' treehouse—
well into the darkness—with emergent

bodies, provocatively foreign, offering glimpses of
geopolitical omnipotence. The bluffing would grow

droll, like playing croquet with swan
eggs—the trajectories were amusing. What

rough beast, its hour come round
at last, slouches toward Jerusalem to

be born? Poetry has been moved
to aisle 12, between the get-well

cards and the pantyhose. Consumers are
understandably tentative. No entertainment epic without

its penumbra of bombs, potholes, belly-up
malls, the barely biographic world where

private poems struggle towards print, out
of a forgettable compost of dim

photographs of the Butler Art Gallery
anxiously snapped in the small rain

of childhood. Memory's verdict is not
guilty, not even there, but the

trial will reconvene tomorrow under blind,
bright sun. The aesthetic forecast calls

for site-specific landfills, while the headlines
define legibility, hurling the first and

biggest stone every morning, smashing glass
houses anew in a song cycle

of entranced voyeurism, clear as a
Senate hearing witnessed by Clark Kent's

x-ray vision. One among others, itself
an other, this body has for

its world the dissed unplanned indies
of the new world order, a

perfect climate and exploding market for
resentment, giving irony an endlessly second

chance to dart its forked tongue
over the sky, covering it with

an Art Deco card of ocher,
pyramidal clouds. Media ladles empty into

the slots every hour as crackdowns
leave deserts to dry in Milwaukee,

Baghdad, St. Petersburg. People starve, while
private lives hunger for significance. Preludes,

Probes and Infinities, Patriots and Wild
Weasels form fast-moving walls of feedback

and commercial self-criticism in the republic
where self-evident bodies stand for nothing

not personally buyable. Art conspiracies wither
on vines as they dangle deep

in the economic understory, or they
fall into categories crude as ashtrays

brought home from clay class. Each
word here is a survivor of

the editorial glare of the biological
father typing letters in the light,

mutagenic present, hoping and fearing to
find absolute resemblance. This nest of

non-natural sounds is the mother of
its own expression, gilding its words

with the sprechtstimme of reading, birdlike
pronunciation in the wreathed trellis of

a working brain on streets where
construction's hand is ever at its

bloodless lips, bidding adieu, adios, sayonara.
While I write, I can watch

this far, unrecognizable cry from direct
desire stand in these lines in

the edge of the paper ocean,
the swirl of infotainment and toxic

profit-taking foaming over its ankles and
sucking back. Then it plunges, objectified.

CHRONIC MEANINGS

for Lee Hickman

The single fact is matter.
Five words can say only.
Black sky at night, reasonably.
I am, the irrational residue.

Blown up chain link fence.
Next morning stronger than ever.
Midnight the pain is almost.
The train seems practically expressive.

A story familiar as a.
Society has broken into bands.
The nineteenth century was sure.
Characters in the withering capital.

The heroic figure straddled the.
The clouds enveloped the tallest.
Tens of thousands of drops.
The monster struggled with Milton.

On our wedding night I.
The sorrow burned deeper than.
Grimly I pursued what violence.
A trap, a catch, a.

Fans stand up, yelling their.
Lights go off in houses.
A fictional look, not quite.
To be able to talk.

The coffee sounds intriguing but.
She put her cards on.
What had been comfortable subjectivity.
The lesson we can each.

Not enough time to thoroughly.
Structure announces structure and takes.
He caught his breath in.
The vista disclosed no immediate.

Alone with a pun in.
The clock face and the.
Rock of ages, a modern.
I think I had better.

Now this particular mall seemed.
The bag of groceries had.
Whether a biographical junkheap or.
In no sense do I.

These fields make me feel.
Mount Rushmore in a sonnet.
Some in the party tried.
So it's not as if.

That always happened until one.
She spread her arms and.
The sky if anything grew.
Which left a lot of.

No one could help it.
I ran farther than I.
That wasn't a good one.
Now put down your pencils.

They won't pull that over.
Standing up to the Empire.
Stop it, screaming in a.
The smell of pine needles.

Economics is not my strong.
Until one of us reads.
I took a breath, then.
The singular heroic vision, unilaterally.

Voices imitate the very words.
Bed was one place where.
A personal life, a toaster.
Memorized experience can't be completely.

The impossibility of the simplest.
So shut the fucking thing.
Now I've gone and put.
But that makes the world.

The point I am trying.
Like a cartoon worm on.
A physical mouth without speech.
If taken to an extreme.

The phone is for someone.
The next second it seemed.
But did that really mean.
Yet Los Angeles is full.

Naturally enough I turn to.
Some things are reversible, some.
You don't have that choice.
I'm going to Jo's for.

Now I've heard everything, he.
One time when I used.
The amount of dissatisfaction involved.
The weather isn't all it's.

You'd think people would have.
Or that they would invent.
At least if the emotional.
The presence of an illusion.

Symbiosis of home and prison.
Then, having become superfluous, time.
One has to give to.
Taste: the first and last.

I remember the look in.
It was the first time.
Some gorgeous swelling feeling that.
Success which owes its fortune.

Come what may it can't.
There are a number of.
But there is only one.
That's why I want to.

A LITERAL TRANSLATION OF VIRGIL'S FOURTH ECLOGUE

Washingtonian[1] Muses, let's roll up our sleaze,[2]
and invest in the grandest theme

park of them all: the past,
as basic and embodied as Fess Parker's

---

1. "Sicilian" in the original; in the original-original,
"Sicelides." "Washingtonian" is an upsidedown synecdoche

(so to speak): a false-toned part
of a false whole in the service,

finally, of something a little less false,
or so I like to think.

2. Puns usually announce (denounce) the excess
of organization in language. This one gestures

in the opposite direction; it's pretty random.
It's hard to believe I feel

compelled to notify people that "Washington
is sleazy," and certainly there are more

direct and convincing ways to do that.
This piece is an inverted pun,

asserting two very different things are identical.
Perhaps the desire to be wrong

is the heart of wanting to write.
There must be some pleasure there.

coonskin cap.[3] If a man is wearing
another animal's tail on his head

his emotions aren't to be dismissed,
even if his speech sounds like he'll

never finish chewing Ma's final biscuit
enough to swallow it all the way.[4]

Never mind his noises, they're only
one of history's running gags: the back

door may creak at midnight, but meanwhile
the whole house has been repossessed.

The feelings in Fess's script are
as difficult to deflect as a hungry

———————————

3. Do people remember Fess Parker? He played
Disney's Davy Crockett, America's original libertarian.

4. I find it odd the way
'subject matter' (sic) creeps into this writing.

Somehow the couplets commit me to continuity
—one could hardly call it narrative;

the areas of most interest (to me
anyway) seemingly begin as sideways moments.

I compare the past to Fess Parker's
coonskin cap: suddenly like the proverbial

chicken hypnotized by a straight line,
I find myself focusing on Fess Parker.

ghost or loan officer. Let the world
remain imperfect food; let the mossy

stream in back of his Tennessee[5] cabin
choke in a few decades with

the wastes of a single narrowly
chiselled narrative; let each wine-dark tree hide

its Disney savage in defiance of history's
singularity; but this copyrighted archetypal whiskey-drinking

typo-fighting individual—Fess Parker is only
one of his many names—will remain

centered in time's freshly baked diorama.

----

5. Doesn't Stevens' "Anecdote of The Jar"
—"I placed a jar in Tennessee, / and

round it was, upon a hill" —
anticipate the current Biosphere (the dystopic Eden

where scientists are spending two years in
a sealed-off greenhouse)? But "Tennessee" doesn't

say this, without my overdetermined reading.
Art, I want to say, saw teeth

rasping at my branch, is not separate.
I can hear those Disney basses

now, those archaic corporate muses, chanting,
"Born on a mountain top in Ten-nes-see. . . ."

Now he squints into the sun, watching

the golf ball he's hit halfway
to Singapore disappear into the cloudless sky

to thunderous applause. There is no need
to be anxious over the path

of the ball or over the fate
of this tableau:[6] in a few

---

6. But of course I am anxious.
Why else the footnotes? I began one

poem years back: "Ed Meese is not
relentless necessity." Soon (or already perhaps)

I'll have to worry if people know
the name. Mr. Memory might answer:

"Ed Meese was District Attorney of Oakland,
California when Ronald Reagan was governor.

When Reagan became President, Meese was
his Attorney General and had a particularly

partisan sense of duty. He chaired
the Meese Commission on Pornography." This poem

is a reaction to the religious right's
authoritarianism based on transcendent language (the

bumpersticker puts it: "God said it. I
believe it. That settles it,") and

fear of labile pleasure. The poem,
then, is a place of such pleasure?

Counting to six and seven as I
try to clear the ground for

my desire for pleasure?? (Labile, the man
said, make mine labile.) Who is

Mr. Memory? Mr. Memory himself might say:
"I was a character in Hitchcock's

The 39 Steps. An idiot savant, I
could remember phenomenal amounts of data

and was used as a transmission
device by German spies in World War

Two, though without knowing what I was
doing. (You could call me Ion

[from the *Ion* of Plato, where
the rhapsode, the reciter of the Muses'

blueprint is ultimately without knowledge, the merest
conduit] —I feel that I need

to make these things clear. Otherwise—
lability. Also, if you'll remember the movie,

I couldn't help but spew facts
when asked.) After some decades of writing,

there comes a point when the contours

of one's verbal habits cease to

surprise. Or is it quite the opposite?
—that a certain doppleganger keeps coming

back, one's own unowned nameless body,
in verbs, vocabulary, linebreaks, no pushing it

away by storms of invention, inventories, concentration,
'the magic hand of chance,' thinking

with the words as they appear,
the dictionary's icestorm lying shattered and bright

in the morning sun you'd think
the inner dome of heaven had fallen

—I had to look that up:
Robert Frost. Who cares! A world without

a ground of repetition is a world
without poetry. I, Mr. Memory—remember?—

died at the end, in cold
Hitchcockian denouement, too fast to seem quite

final at first, and the secret
of the noiseless engine remained hidden inside

my small fictional body. I never talked
anything like this, it's only because

I was asked that I'm forced
to ride the rails of this answer."

centuries (or days, it makes no
difference) Fess Parker may be unknown, squeezed

onto a magnetic card of 1950's America
and its actors playing colonial heroes,

his terms as President only remembered
by over- or under-paid specialists, but this

is a prophetic poem, Virgil's 4th eclogue,[7]
and the principal attribute of such

canonical utterance is its perpetual freshness.
Time stands still and meaning is everywhere.[8]

It's shocking but true: I'm translating literally;[9]

---

7. Christian thinkers considered Virgil's 4th eclogue
(37 B.C.) a prophecy of Christ's birth.

8. I like it when the couplets
come out even. (Assuming 13 is even.)

(But how to imagine a poem touching
a specific time many centuries later?)

9. I'd thought about claiming this was
a literal translation a few hours ago.

Half-thoughts were flitting about happily in single-winged
narcissistic swoops in the half-lit belfry:

I would quote the Latin. Push irony
to its ecstatic death in lie.

At tibi prima, puer, nullo munuscula cultu
errantis hederas passim cum baccare tellus

which my eye fell upon just now
by chance would be good because

of its structure of one seven word
and one six word line, like

these couplets. I wanted to say
that the quoted Latin was a translation,

a literal one, from the original
Latin. At one point I half-wanted to

refer to the original printer's error in
Canto XIII, which has since been

corrected without Pound's permission. When Kenner
pointed it out to him, he dismissed

the problem, saying, Repeat in XIII
sanctioned by time and the author, or

rather first by the author, who
never objects to the typesetter making improvements:

And even I can remember / A day
when historians left blanks in their

/ writings, I mean for things they
didn't know, / But that time seems to

in fact, not only are these

Virgil's exact words, the sounds are identical
as well. Reading this, you are

reading the original Latin, a contingency
that I, Virgil, foresaw[10] as I wrote:

———————————

be passing." / I mean for things
they didn't know, / But that time seems

to be passing." If I had
any vocabulary (never mind the knowledge I

guess!—first things first) from computer programming,
I could make specific reference to

something like recursive instructions: the original
Latin would say to quote the original

Latin in the translation. I should acknowledge
the Monty Pythonesque qualities of these

'thoughts'. (That's not to say they're not
original——at least I think they

are.) Burroughs' sense of the word
as virus is hovering in the vicinity.

10. At this point, I've decided to try
footnotes as a way to react

to this piece: it feels strange enough
to merit such measures. Perhaps this

At tibi prima, puer, nullo munuscula cultu
errantis hederas passim cum baccare tellus

as well as its rough translation—
But to you, first, child, little gifts

from the uncultivated earth, wandering ivy
with its berries (perhaps a hint there

in baccare of Bacchus and state power
torn apart and eaten by orgasmic

women out from under the so-called thumb)—[11]
This has been written already in

_____

equal strangeness will create some balance.
For the record: this was the first

footnote (originally written in prose, though I'm
currently rewriting it in couplets, as

well as adding to it), but
the poem 'itself' mocks origins and records.

11. The violence of oppositional sexuality that
most authorities fear takes a cornucopia of

forms—face and voice altered, social
markers shown as flesh and unanchored expression

—isn't flesh something that gets *eaten?*
Chew, grind, tongue the pulp, taste—splashed

to pieces like a visual stick
in water at the moment the bodies

the original because, with the birth
of the ruling child,[12] time becomes circular.

_____

become, as Harlequin romances like to write,
"one"—but the violence of state

sexuality is the oneness of that oneness,
mythic marriage with all the trimmings

—Bush opposing the species diversification treaty,
saying in the Fess-Parker-gone-to-college accent that if

they think I'm going to do anything
to hurt the American family . . . is

it always state eyes that stare
at Miss March photogenically licking Miss April

and the invisible hand of the marketplace
that rubs its thumb and forefinger

together with only the glossy paper
intervening? Looking out of the poem's eternally

framing open window at this week's
breaking glass, I see our nation, pinnacled

atop its past: Macedonia, Rome, England, Cambodia
—remember those pyramids of intellectual skulls?

12. There's a crucial possibility open here:
I'm really tempted to write ruling-class child.

The eclogue can certainly be read
as an egregious piece of flattery: Virgil

75

owes his leisure to Maecenas, Augustus's
minister of culture more or less; this

dependence leads him to write the *Aeneid*
as an epic in the service

of state power, transmogrifying Homer's oral-based
aristocratic-communal technique into the protocol for imperial

pedagogy and angst for isolate authors.
The fourth eclogue is often preposterous under

the strain of laying utopic pleasantries
at the feet of a state official

(Pollio, apparently) who had just become
a father. I.e.: This is the ultimate

age foretold by the Sibyl's prophecy. . .
the Golden Age returns . . . it's while you,

Anne Imelda Radice, are consul that
this holy age begins. The child will

live a godlike life, and see
the gods . . . he'll rule a world pacified

by his father's virtue. . . . Goats will walk
home untended with full udders, oxen

no longer fear lions, snakes will die . . .
the ram will dye his own

That circle has been completed in footnote
12, letting me step outside to

_____

fleece now yellow, now purple, grazing lambs
willingly shall turn their wool red,

you won't need your wallet, full-time childcare,
snorkeling, handsome Caribbean waiters smiling beside

roast beef, shrimp and quartered pineapples.
But I respond to the poem, too,

especially the end: Begin, little child,
recognize your mother, smile at her, she

underwent ten tedious months, begin, little child:
if you don't smile at your

parents you'll never be worthy of
sharing the feast of a god, or

the bed of a goddess—Freud!
where *were* you when *that* got written!

Despite the sycophancy, the poem has
a charge: pleasure and love are at

the root of the intelligible world,
and the potentialities that flow from that

are just and beatific. That happiness
animates Virgil's conditional claim near the end:

if the utmost of life was available
to him, and if he could

these words I wrote thirteen years ago:
Steal a few moments from the

running time Max shoving himself against
the netting of his playpen finds himself

his bottle now standing on the back
of his busybox toppled twice now

standing stooping down two hands raising
his bottle on high aria furiosa long

notes held searched through some blocks hang
off the railing he puts them

in his mouth and sighs pulls himself
up wooden bead on a string

in his mouth tasted dropped eyed
at arm's length he leans back and

groans at the ceiling chanting pulsing O's
until he begins to jump now

a forefinger in the mouth to chew
and modify the noise waving and

a falsetto yodel picks up spits out
the bottle crawls in a circle

———————————

sing the fact of this child
with sufficient inspiration, then he would be

a better poet that either Apollo
or Pan: that's an interesting human claim.

spits picks it up drinks embraces the
basketball and rolls over goes go

go go as he hits his
wooden nails with his hand stands at

the railing going Da da Da
jumping looking over his shoulder short plaintive

hums escaping almost whining he reaches up
to the doorknob on the other

side rattles the door staring up
to the top using his strength jumping

talking a brief emphatic silence then
a yell he turns away then sits

walks across the mess to this side
again begins pulling up the mat

staring at the fiberboard underneath a few
glissando squeals now some O's as

he stares at and touches the metal
tube brace standing again feels the

shiny chrome bolts at the top
hangs down by his arms head back

up to the ceiling he almost falls
over swings sideways does fall down

cries his bottle's stuck between the webbing
and the floor he gets it

out drinks deep breathing hard holds it
at arm's length bangs his fallen

busybox drinks again stares at and fingers
the nipple a moment of quiet

while he farts backs away squeals
spits goes yay grabs it drinks throws

it down spits propeller noise from
his lips stares at me pulls himself

up standing at the railing on top
of his busybox falsetto yodel now

large modulated calls out to space
staring at his feet as he slides

one along the smooth cardboard back
of the busybox which squeaks he crows

turns it with difficulty back over
picks the thing up hits with it

drops it picks up the pink pig
nailbrush puts it in his mouth[13]

---

13. Imagine writing that would make good
its second by second letter by letter

birth and existence as if the body
moving made spaces it could understand.